Contents

Roman Britain 4

A Fighting Machine 6

A Roman Fort 8

A Soldier's Life 10

Roads and Chariots 12

A Roman Townhouse 14

Mosaics and Crafts 16

The Latest Fashion 18

Childhood 20

In the Kitchen 22

A Roman Dinner Party 24

At the Baths 26

Timeline 28

Glossary 29

Activities 30

Finding Out More 31

Index 32

Roman Britain

In AD 43, an army of over 40,000 soldiers landed in Kent, on the east coast of Britain. It had been sent from Rome by the Emperor Claudius, who wanted Britain to become part of the mighty Roman Empire. By this time, the Roman Empire stretched across most of Europe and into North Africa.

The invading Roman army was highly organized. It was divided into units of 80 soldiers each, called centuries. Each century was commanded by a centurion. The soldiers in each century were called 'legionaries'. Among them were *signifers*, who carried the army's standards, and *cornicens*, who sent signals by blowing on bronze horns.

Roman legionaries look out over the landscape of Britain.

Signifer wearing bearskin

Standard

Centurion

Legionary

Medals

Cornicen with bronze horn

THE ROMANS

RECONSTRUCTED

Jason Hook
Photographs by Martyn F. Chillmaid

RECONSTRUCTED

Other titles in this series:
**The Home Front • The Saxons and Vikings
The Tudors • The Victorians**

Conceived and produced for Hodder Wayland by

Nutshell
MEDIA

Intergen House, 65–67 Western Road, Hove BN3 2JQ, UK
www.nutshellmedialtd.co.uk

© Copyright 2003 Nutshell Media

Editor: Polly Goodman
Designer: Simon Borrough
All reconstructions set up and photographed by: Martyn F. Chillmaid

First published in Great Britain in 2003 by Hodder Wayland,
an imprint of Hodder Children's Books.
Reprinted in 2004
This paperback edition published by Wayland in 2007,
an imprint of Hachette Children's Books.

British Library Cataloguing in Publication Data
Hook, Jason
The Romans. – (Reconstructed)
– Social life and customs – Pictorial works – Juvenile literature
I. Title
937'.06'0222

ISBN-10: 0 7502 4993 5
ISBN-13: 978 0 7502 4993 5

Printed and bound in China

Hachette Children's Books
338 Euston Road, London NW1 3BH

Cover photographs: main photo: Firing an *onager*; from top to bottom:
a family in the *triclinium* (dining room); a slave and her mistress in the kitchen; a centurion;
a father and son in the *peristilium* (courtyard); a mosaic craftsman at work.

Title page: Relaxing with a Samian cup of wine.

The legionaries found a land very different from the busy towns back home. The country was inhabited by warring tribes of Britons, who lived in small, circular huts of wood and clay, with thatched roofs. Their settlements were simple clearings, surrounded by ditches, and fences made from wooden stakes. From wooden watchtowers, sentries kept a look-out for attacks by enemy tribes.

Roof thatched with straw

Wooden stakes

Watchtower

A settlement typical of the Britons.

The Britons were ferocious warriors who rode into battle in chariots, hurling javelins. But they were no match for the disciplined Roman legionaries, who won battle after battle.

Gradually, the Roman armies took control of England and Wales, creating a province of the Empire that they called Britannia. Over the next 350 years, the Romans would build cities with law-courts, temples and public baths; villas with central heating and mosaic floors; market places filled with luxury goods from Europe; and stone roads that stretched for hundreds of kilometres across the landscape.

A Fighting Machine

Roman legionaries in the 'tortoise' formation.

Curved shield

Viewing gap

Iron or bronze boss

Leather sandals

Rigid discipline, careful organization and clever tactics made the Roman legionaries fearsome opponents in battle. When faced with enemy missiles, legionaries sometimes joined together beneath their shields. This formation was known as the *testudo*, or tortoise, because the legionaries moved forward very slowly, protected beneath a shell of shields. The *testudo* formation was said to be so strong that you could drive a chariot over it.

The legionaries also had better equipment than their enemies. Their large, rectangular shields were made of wood and leather. They were painted in war-like designs and had an iron or bronze 'boss' at their centre.

As well as his shield, a legionary was protected by the lightweight plates of armour he wore over his woollen tunic. The legionary's helmet protected his head, cheeks and neck. He also wore a studded apron to protect his groin.

When the Romans advanced on a hill-fort, they followed an exact plan. First, they terrified their enemy by firing huge, metal bolts from giant crossbows. Occasionally, they also used a catapult to launch rocks at their opponents. This catapult was known as an *onager*, or wild ass, because it kicked like a mule when it was fired.

Next, the legionaries advanced, protected by the *testudo* formation. Opening out into a line, they hurled javelins at their enemy. Then they attacked in a tight formation, battering their enemies with the fronts of their shields. From behind this wall of shields, each of the close-packed legionaries made short, deadly thrusts with his short sword, called a *gladius*, or his dagger. Even when the well-drilled legionaries were outnumbered, such a disciplined attack was too powerful for the brave but disorganized Britons.

Plate armour

Helmet with face and neck guards

Woollen tunic

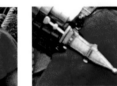
Dagger in scabbard

Gladius in scabbard

Catapult cradle

Basket of rocks

Lever

The firing of an *onager*.

A Roman Fort

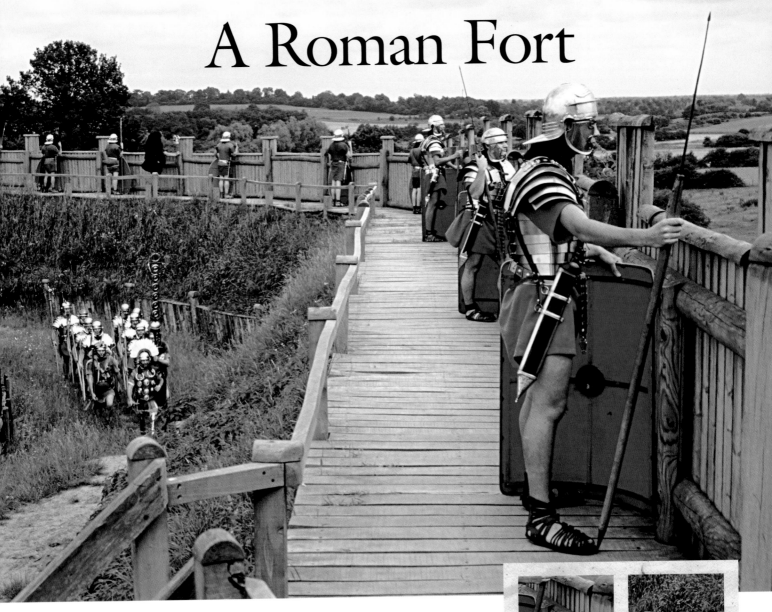

Sentries stand guard at a Roman fort.

As they settled into life in Britain, the Roman legions built the forts that would become their homes. These forts offered vital protection against the hostile tribes, known as barbarians, who marauded across Scotland and Wales.

To build the four walls of a fort, first the legionaries dug a ditch and piled up the earth behind it to form a bank. Everything was done with typical Roman precision. The bank was covered with turf cut into pieces measuring exactly 18 x 12 inches (45 cm x 30 cm). Along the top, the legionaries constructed wooden ramparts.

Wooden ramparts   **Turf bank**

Sentry   **Patrol**

On top of the fort's ramparts ran a walkway, along which sentries could patrol. On each side of the fort there was a gateway, with a second, higher rampart above it. From here, sentries could not only keep watch, but also hurl missiles down on attackers threatening the gates.

Stepping into the fort was a bit like entering a Roman town. Streets were laid out in an exact grid, and on either side of them stood various buildings. In the workshops, a blacksmith set his furnace blazing, and wagons and carts were repaired. Inside the fort headquarters, the legion's sacred standards were kept, alongside the equally precious chest containing the legionaries' wages. A hospital contained an operating room for the surgeon; and a granary was built with raised floors to keep grain safe from damp and rats.

The fort's barracks were large enough to house thousands of men. A group of eight legionaries slept in a single room, and kept all their equipment in another. A centurion had the luxury of four rooms to himself, while the fort commander had his own house.

Outside the fort's walls, local traders soon established a cluster of shops and taverns. There was also a bath-house, built outside the fort because of the danger of fire from the furnace that heated the water. In the bath-house, the legionaries not only washed, but relaxed and forgot about their many duties.

The two-storey defence at a fort's gateway.

Sentry

Double gates

Ladder to higher ramparts

A Soldier's Life

The Romans enlisted thousands of soldiers from the lands that they conquered. These soldiers were called auxiliaries. Among the auxiliaries who invaded Britain were boatmen from Iraq and archers from Syria. Many strong Britons also joined the Roman army. If an auxiliary survived long enough to serve in the army for 25 years, he received a special reward: a bronze certificate making him a Roman citizen.

New recruits practised their fighting skills with wooden staves instead of swords, heavy wickerwork shields, and weapons filled with weights to build up their muscles.

Auxiliary soldiers practise their fighting skills.

Legionary

Wickerwork shield

Hob-nailed sandal

Auxiliary

Woollen tunic

Studded apron

Leather satchel   Flask

Javelin   Bronze mess tin

Training also involved plenty of marching. The Roman legions were famous for their ability to move faster and further than their enemies, and the centurion lashed out with his vinewood staff at any slackers. A legionary had to be able to march 30 km in five hours, carrying a pack weighing 20 kg. He wore sandals with iron nails in the soles to make them hardwearing, which beat out a rhythm as the legion marched in time along a stone road. A popular nickname for legionaries was Marius's mules, after the Roman general Marius, who forced his soldiers to carry their own equipment rather than have it transported by cart.

On his shoulder, the legionary rested his equipment strapped to a pole, rather like a hod-carrier transporting bricks. It included tools and wooden stakes for making a fortified camp. A leather satchel contained spare clothes and personal belongings – perhaps a letter from home, or some dice for gambling away the evenings. There was also a flask filled with sour wine, the bronze 'mess tin' from which the legionary ate, and a string bag for carrying food. Bread, beans, onions, lentils and salted fish might make up his rations.

The equipment of a marching legionary.

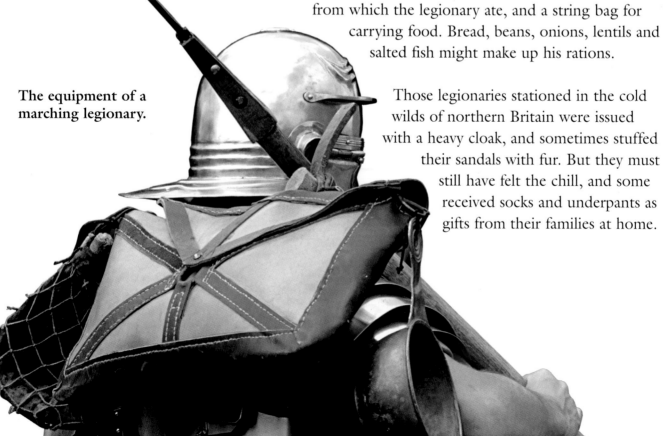

Those legionaries stationed in the cold wilds of northern Britain were issued with a heavy cloak, and sometimes stuffed their sandals with fur. But they must still have felt the chill, and some received socks and underpants as gifts from their families at home.

Roads and Chariots

When the Romans arrived in Britain, the only routes were little more than dirt tracks. They immediately set to work on a programme of road building. Long, straight roads were plotted by army surveyors at first, then dug out by labourers under the watchful eye of an army engineer. Finally, they were filled with deep foundations of sand and local stone.

The Roman road at Blackstone Edge, Lancashire.

Paving stones

Kerb stones

Gutter

Most roads were covered with gravel, but one surviving example, at Blackstone Edge in the Pennines, has a paved surface and kerb stones. On hills, the road has a gutter at the centre, where the driver of a heavy, ox-drawn cart could press down a brake-pole. This would prevent his cart rolling back down the slope and allow the oxen a well-earned rest before continuing the climb.

Spina

Whip

Wheel flying loose

Chariot

Rider falling off

All manner of travellers used the new roads, from traders transporting their goods, to legions marching between forts. The Romans also had a postal service, the *Cursus Publicus*, whose couriers galloped from city to city carrying messages.

Stone columns called milestones were placed at the roadside every Roman mile (1.4 km). Carvings on these stones showed travellers the distance to the nearest city. There were also special post-houses every 20 km or so, where couriers could swap their tired horses for fresh ones.

Chariot-racing, shown on a mosaic from a villa in Britain.

One form of horse-drawn transport provided the Romans with one of their favourite entertainments – chariot-racing. This spectator sport was extremely popular, and people supported one of four teams (Reds, Whites, Blues or Greens). In Rome, races took place in a huge stadium called the Circus Maximus. In Britain, circuits were probably just marked out on an area of flat ground. Mosaics in Britain show chariot-racers with whips careering around a long barrier called the *spina* (meaning 'backbone'), with horses tumbling to the ground, chariots swerving and wheels flying loose.

A Roman Townhouse

Britain's first towns sprang up soon after the Roman invasion. They had carefully planned streets, running water and sewers. Wealthy families lived in comfortable townhouses, with five or six rooms facing on to a private courtyard garden, called the *peristilium*.

The *peristilium* featured paved paths wide enough for two people to stroll side by side and arrangements of shrubs, herb and flower beds, and fish ponds. Roses and lilies were popular flowers. Among them stood statues of gods and emperors, to seek their blessing over the household.

Statue   Slave   Pond   Flower beds   Herb garden

A family in the garden of a townhouse.

A slave builds a fire to heat the kitchen oven.

Many townhouses had glazed windows, painted walls and ceilings, and mosaic floors. The slaves did all the cooking in the kitchen, using an oven for roasting and baking. Keeping this lit was just one of the slaves' many tasks.

Firewood

Dried herbs

Oven

Earth floor

Wealthy families had a number of slaves. They were the property of the household and were unprotected by law. In the countryside, some slaves were terribly mistreated and had their children killed. But in the towns, many domestic slaves enjoyed a comfortable life. Their lodgings, clothing and food were all provided, and they became trusted and valued members of the family.

In a townhouse, a slave might play many roles: cook, cleaner, lady's-maid, hairdresser, nursemaid, and sometimes simply companion. Favourite slaves were greatly valued, and there are a number of surviving tombstones erected in memory of a beloved slave by a grateful master.

Mosaics and Crafts

A mosaic craftsman in his workshop.

Only the richest people could afford to lay mosaic floors in their townhouse, and they soon became fashionable symbols of wealth and status. Mosaic workers kept workshops in the forum, where they cut out small stones called *tesserae*. The broad range of stone in Britain – white chalk, grey limestone, yellow sandstone, red ironstone and black slate – was ideal for creating the different colours needed to form a mosaic.

Mosaics were unknown in Britain until the Romans came. At first, only Roman craftworkers could make them, but Britons working as apprentices gradually learned the trade and set up their own workshops.

Tesserae

Stone bench

Hammer

Saw

Chisel

Set squares

Making a mosaic floor was a skilled and painstaking process. First, the master craftsman drew up his design on a scroll, and presented it to the house owner. Then he calculated the size, shape and colours needed, and set to work with his apprentices cutting tens of thousands of *tessarae*. Some mosaics for border panels were also made in the workshop.

At the townhouse, the mosaic makers laid a layer of cement and scratched their design on to it. Then they laid a sticky bed of lime and water, into which the *tessarae* were pressed. Set squares and rulers were used to position them exactly. Finally, when the mosaic was completed, it was polished to bring out its full glory.

Throughout the Roman Empire, mosaics formed similar pictures: the proud heads of gods, characters from plays, geometric patterns, and magnificent birds and beasts.

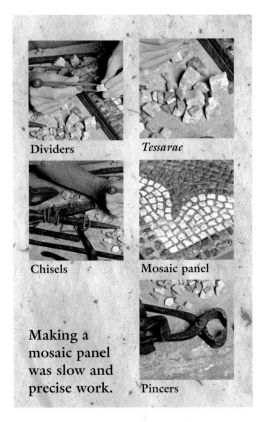

Dividers

Tessarae

Chisels

Mosaic panel

Making a mosaic panel was slow and precise work.

Pincers

The Latest Fashion

Fashion and beauty were a serious matter in Roman townhouses. A slave dressing her mistress had the help of several tools: curling irons, combs and hairpins to style hair; tweezers for plucking eyebrows; a scoop to remove ear-wax; files to manicure fingernails; spoons to apply perfumed oils from flasks and pots; and a mirror of polished metal so that her work could be admired. Hairstyles were quite elaborate, with long hair pinned up in plaits and curls. Some dark-haired ladies preferred to wear wigs made from the blonde hair of their slave girls!

A fashionable woman wore make-up of chalk or white lead to lighten her face and arms; red ochre to brighten her cheeks; and eyeshadow made from ash. To prolong her beauty, she might use face-packs of bread and milk. False teeth were also available.

A slave arranges her mistress's hair.

Hair plait

Necklace

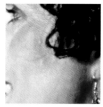
Red-ochre rouge

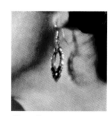
Earring

Powdered-ash eyeshadow

Painted ceiling

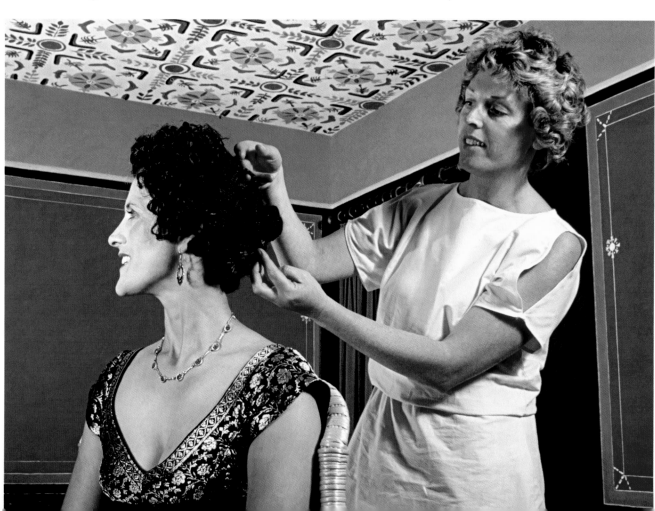

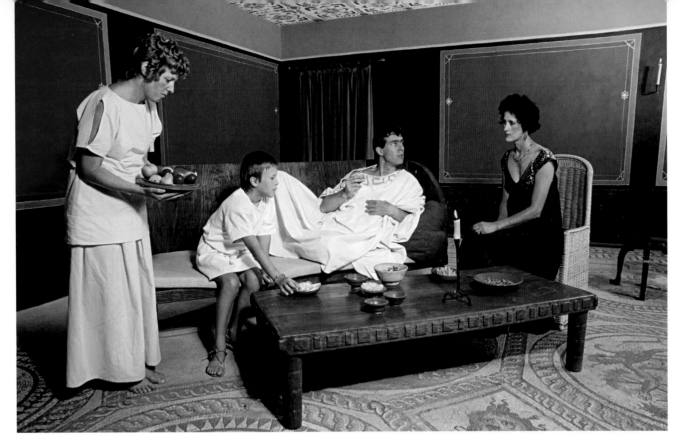

Tunic

Stola

Toga

Embroidered dress

Sandal

A family and their slave dressed for dinner.

Women wore a long tunic called a *stola*, made of wool or linen, with a shorter tunic over the top. For special occasions this might be made from expensive cloth and embroidered. Ornate brooches were used both to fasten clothes and simply for decoration. Necklaces and earrings were also popular, in gold, silver and precious stones for the wealthy, and bone, glass or pottery for the poor.

Both men and women wore sandals around the house and at the baths, and leather boots when going out. Men wore one or more short tunics beneath the most distinctive Roman garment: the toga. This was a huge piece of woollen cloth that was draped about the wearer, then thrown over the shoulder. Slaves had to be trained in the tricky art of dressing their master in his toga.

Childhood

Childhood did not last long in Roman times. From the age of 7, a son was expected to follow his father everywhere, finding out about his business affairs and learning how to behave.

Until he completed his education, a boy wore a toga with a purple border. The purple border represented a barrier protecting his innocence. When he was 16, the boy offered this toga to the gods in a special ceremony. He then received the plain white toga of an adult, had his first shave, and was given an adult haircut.

Plain white toga

Short-sleeved tunic

Purple border

Sandal

A father and his son in their togas.

The purple border of the toga was one of many superstitions the Romans held about protecting a child. Nine days after a boy or girl was born, they were given a locket of leather or gold, called a *bulla*. The locket was filled with charms that were believed to keep the child safe. Parents also asked for the help of the household gods, who were represented as statues. These were set in altars in the house where both a parent and a child could offer sacrifices, such as pieces of food. When a boy reached manhood, he would sacrifice his *bulla* to the gods that had led him safely through childhood.

Children grew up under the protection of the family slaves. In a wealthy family, a child might have a slave nursemaid and an educated Greek slave to help with studies. An older slave would escort the child to school, which was usually in a room at the forum. A slave who could entertain children with music was highly valued. Children were given lessons in dancing and playing the *cithara*, a musical instrument like a small harp or lyre. It had a deep sound-box to increase the volume, and up to eleven strings tuned with pegs.

A slave entertains her master's son.

Cithara

Tuning pegs

Sound-box

Household god in altar

Children also had toys to keep them amused. These included rattles shaped like animals, jointed wooden dolls, hoops and spinning tops, see-saws and swings. Some children had toy chariots, which they harnessed to mice and birds to imitate their chariot-racing heroes.

In the Kitchen

In townhouse kitchens, local produce such as hares and pigeons hung on the walls, while spices were kept in storage pots. The pots had the name of their contents, and sometimes advertising slogans, scratched on their sides.

Slaves used chopping tools ranging from iron-bladed cleavers to bronze pastry-cutters. A pestle and mortar were used to grind up spices. Food was cooked in bronze or earthenware pots. These were placed on a gridiron over a raised hearth, and heated by charcoal burnt in the hollows of tiles.

Many of the items in the kitchen were imported from abroad, then purchased at the local market. Pottery was imported from Gaul (France) in enormous quantities, particularly the red Samian ware, on which any fashionable family would serve food to its guests. The wine that was drunk with the meal, and the olive oil in which food was cooked, were shipped in from Spain, Greece, Italy and Gaul. They were transported in thin-necked storage jars, called *amphorae*.

A slave receives instructions from her mistress in the kitchen.

Hare   Wood pigeons

Dried thyme   Grid-iron

Cleaver   Duck eggs

Cooking pot   Storage jars

Ginger

Garlic

Rosemary

Peppercorns

Amphora   Parsley   Mint   Onions   Bay leaves   Sage

**Roman pottery
vessels with herbs
and spices.**

Food did not always reach the kitchen completely fresh, so herbs, spices and sauces were used to disguise the taste. A strong fish sauce called *liquamen* was particularly popular. It was made from rotting fish guts, strong herbs and plenty of salt, and the Romans adored it.

Herbs such as bay leaves, parsley, rosemary and sage were all used in Roman cooking, as were spices. Ginger, shipped in from Africa, was very popular, but it was pepper that really made the Romans' mouths water. Peppercorns were used to liven up sauces and sprinkled over main courses. They were even used in desserts to flavour custards and fruits.

A Roman Dinner Party

In a Roman townhouse, the evening meal was served in the *triclinium* (dining room). Wealthy Romans loved to turn dining into a party, and often invited friends. Guests lay on low, wooden couches, propping themselves up on striped cushions stuffed with straw. Spoons and knives were used, but there were no forks. Mostly, people ate with their fingers, and dinner could be a very messy affair.

At a typical Roman dinner party, a mixture of cheap wine with honey or water, called *muslum*, was drunk during the meal. More expensive wines were kept for after-dinner drinking. Drunkenness was common, and a wreath of rose petals was believed to protect the wearer against the effects of too much wine.

Drinking wine at the evening meal.

Amphora filled with *muslum*

Candle

Samian cup

Rose-petal wreath

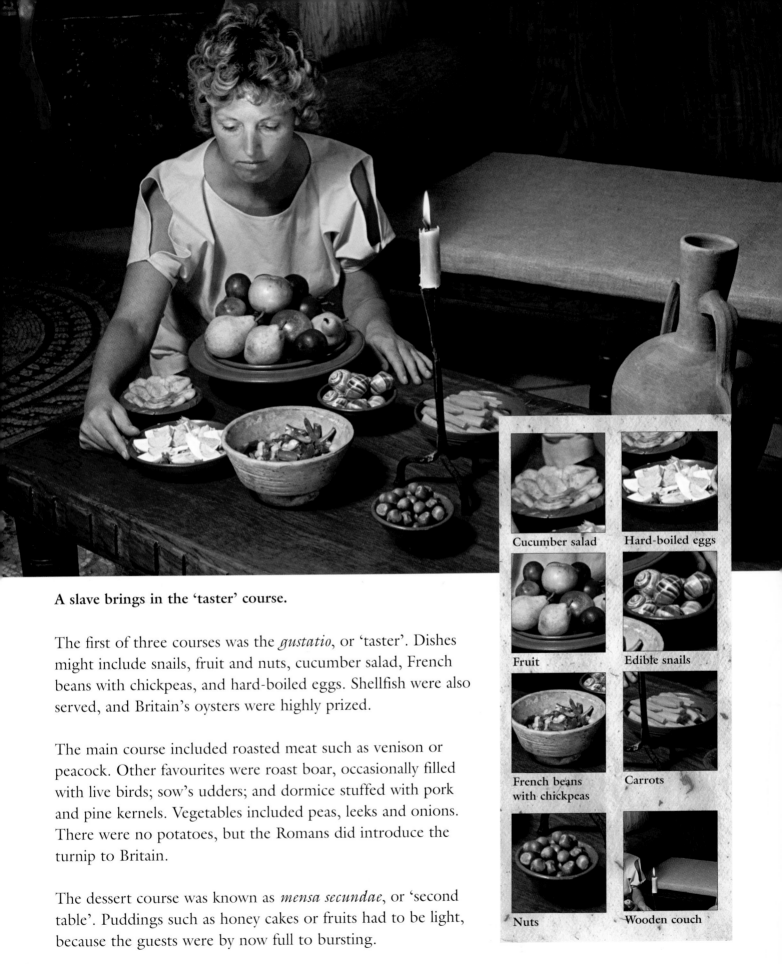

A slave brings in the 'taster' course.

The first of three courses was the *gustatio*, or 'taster'. Dishes might include snails, fruit and nuts, cucumber salad, French beans with chickpeas, and hard-boiled eggs. Shellfish were also served, and Britain's oysters were highly prized.

The main course included roasted meat such as venison or peacock. Other favourites were roast boar, occasionally filled with live birds; sow's udders; and dormice stuffed with pork and pine kernels. Vegetables included peas, leeks and onions. There were no potatoes, but the Romans did introduce the turnip to Britain.

The dessert course was known as *mensa secundae*, or 'second table'. Puddings such as honey cakes or fruits had to be light, because the guests were by now full to bursting.

Cucumber salad

Hard-boiled eggs

Fruit

Edible snails

French beans with chickpeas

Carrots

Nuts

Wooden couch

At the Baths

If the Romans wished to gossip with friends, discuss business, exercise, play games, wash, or just lie back and relax, they headed for the public baths. Roman baths were built all round Britain, and they were among the grandest Roman buildings. Massive pillars carved from local stone held up magnificent ceilings. Heated water was pumped into pools lined with lead, and decorated with beautiful mosaics of gods and sea creatures.

The baths were reserved for women in the morning, while men visited in the afternoon. Visitors would progress through a series of rooms. They would leave their clothes in the *apodyterium* (changing room). Then they might work out in a courtyard called the *palaestra*, where exercise ranged from throwing balls to rolling dice.

Stepping into one of the public baths.

The first bath to enter was the warm *tepidarium*. Then there was the scorching steam of the *caldarium*. The Romans did not use soap, but the bather could ask a slave to rub oil into their skin, and then use an object called a *strigil* to scrape it away along with the day's grime. Finally, the bather could plunge into the freezing water of the *frigidarium*.

Baths featured many examples of Roman invention. Water was supplied across great distances along channels called aqueducts. The floors were raised up on columns of tiles and hot air was pumped beneath them in a system called the *hypocaust*. The same system was also used in villas and houses. Water was drained away through huge sewers, which also flushed out public toilets.

The baths were the finest example of how a Roman invention made possible a new lifestyle in Britain. Reminders of this – villas, baths, mosaics, roads – can still be seen today, allowing us to reconstruct the amazing lives that were lived in Roman Britain over 2,000 years ago.

Channel to furnace

Heated floor

Pillar of tiles

The under-floor heating known as the *hypocaust*.

Timeline

753 BC   According to legend, the city of Rome was founded in this year.

312 BC   The first great Roman road, the Via Appia, is built. The same year, the first Roman aqueduct is built.

55 BC   The Roman Emperor Julius Caesar lands in Britain, but does not conquer the island.

AD 43   An army sent by the Emperor Claudius lands in Britain, and begins the successful Roman invasion of the island.

AD 44   Roman legionaries defeat Britons at Maiden Castle in Dorset.

*c.*AD 50   Roman towns develop in Britain, in places including London, Dorchester, Colchester and St Albans.

AD 60   Britons led by Queen Boudicca stage a rebellion against Roman rule, which is put down by the Roman legions.

*c.*AD 75   The first Roman villas are built in the British countryside.

AD 78   The Roman legions complete the conquest of Wales.

*c.*AD 80   A network of Roman roads across Britain is complete.

AD 122   Work begins on Hadrian's Wall, a massive wall built across the north of Britain to keep the wild barbarians at bay.

AD 212   All free inhabitants of the Roman Empire are allowed to become citizens of Rome.

AD 313   The Emperor Constantine ends the Roman persecution of Christians.

AD 367–9   Barbarians (Picts, Scots and Saxons) launch attacks against Roman Britain.

AD 407   The Roman legions withdraw from Britain to defend Rome.

AD 410   The Roman Emperor Honorius advises Britons to organize their own defences, leading to the end of the age of Roman Britain.

Note: The letter '*c*' is short for *circa*, which is the Latin word meaning 'approximately'. The letters 'BC' and 'AD' refer to the Christian calendar. 'BC' is short for 'Before Christ'. It means the number of years before the birth of Jesus Christ. 'AD' is short for Anno Domini, which is Latin for 'in the year of our Lord.' It means the number of years after the birth of Christ. Something that happened in AD 200 took place 200 years after the year Christ was born.

Glossary

amphora (plural *amphorae*) A jar with a thin neck and two handles used to hold wine and olive oil.

aqueduct An artificial channel used to move water from one place to another.

auxiliaries Foreign soldiers who fought with the Roman army.

barbarians People belonging to tribes outside the Roman Empire.

barracks Housing blocks for soldiers.

boss A rounded stud at the centre of a shield.

centurion An officer in the Roman army, in charge of a century.

century A unit of 80 soldiers in the Roman army.

chariot A two-wheeled vehicle pulled by horses, used for warfare and racing.

cithara A musical instrument like a small harp, popular in Roman times.

cornicens Roman soldiers who sent signals by blowing through curved, bronze horns.

forum The market place at the centre of a Roman town.

geometric Regular lines and patterns.

granary A place for storing grain.

gridiron A frame of metal bars on which food can be cooked over a flame.

hearth The floor of a fireplace.

hypocaust The Roman system of heating, in which hot air is blown beneath a floor.

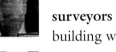

imported Brought into one country from another.

javelin A long, light spear.

legionary A regular soldier in the Roman army.

legions Divisions of 3,000–6,000 legionaries in the Roman army.

liquamen A strong fish sauce.

mosaic A decoration created by arranging many tiny pieces of stone.

onager A type of Roman catapult.

pestle and mortar A blunt tool and bowl used for grinding food.

ramparts The walls of a fort, with a walkway at the top.

set squares Right-angled triangular tools used for measuring accurate angles.

signifers Soldiers in the Roman army who carried the standards, or flags.

standards The flags or symbols of an army.

surveyors People who study land before building work begins.

toga A loose, flowing garment worn by men in Roman times.

villas Large country houses.

vinewood staff The stick carried by a centurion, both as a symbol of his position and as a cane used to discipline legionaries.

Activities

pp4–5 Roman Britain

- Use tracing paper to copy the picture on page 4. Then label it with all the information you can find about the different kinds of Roman soldier.
- Imagine that you are an ancient Briton who has just seen a Roman army arrive with camels and elephants. In a role play with other members of your class, try to describe the terrifying creatures you have just seen to your neighbouring tribes.

pp6–7 A Fighting Machine

- Using a large piece of card, make a model of the Roman shield you can see on page 6. Use paint to copy the designs on it, and a bottle top to make the 'boss'.
- Use the Internet to find some more information about the Roman *onager* you can see on page 7. Write a set of instructions to help somebody fire it for the first time.

pp8–9 A Roman Fort

- Use the information here to draw a plan of a Roman fort, showing where the different buildings will be.
- Write a list of rules for how a legionary should behave in his fort. You might be able to find a real list in a book from your local library.

pp10–11 A Soldier's Life

- Use the Internet to find maps showing the Roman Empire. Draw and colour in your own map, showing the different countries ruled by Rome.
- Imagine that you are a legionary living at a fort in Britain. Write a letter home to your family describing your life and asking for gifts to be sent.

pp12–13 Roads and Chariots

- Imagine that you are a Roman courier travelling across Britain. Write a diary describing the roads and the places that you visit.
- Design a chariot-racing boardgame. Write down the rules of the game, design the counters, and draw a track on some card. Don't forget to include the *spina* and the different-coloured teams.

pp14–15 A Roman Townhouse

- Using the information from the picture on page 14, and from other books about the Romans, use coloured pens and a large piece of card to design a Roman garden.
- Imagine that you are a slave. Write a diary about one day in a townhouse, listing the many different tasks you have to perform.

pp16–17 Mosaics and Crafts

- Study the pictures on pages 16–17 carefully, then try to draw the different tools used by a mosaic craftsman.
- Cut up different-coloured card into tiny pieces, then stick them on to a large piece of card to make your own mosaic picture. Try to copy a Roman design, such as the one shown on page 17.

pp18–19 The Latest Fashion

- Imagine that the Romans had magazines. Write a fashion article describing the latest trends in jewellery and make-up.
- Design a set of clothes for a Roman family. Base it on the photograph on page 19, but add your own special touches. Label the design with the names of different items.